KEEP
CALM
FOR
MUMS

KEEP CALM FOR MUMS

Summersdale Publishers Ltd
46 West Street
Chichester
West Sussex
PO19 1RP
UK

www.summersdale.com

Printed and bound in the Czech Republic

ISBN: 978-1-84953-253-2

Substantial discounts on bulk quantities of Summersdale books are available to corporations, professional associations and other organisations. For details telephone Summersdale Publishers on (+44-1243-771107), fax (+44-1243-786300) or email (nicky@summersdale.com).

KEEP
CALM
FOR
MUMS

Mother is the name
for God in the lips and
hearts of little children.

William Makepeace Thackeray

To describe my
mother would be
to write about a
hurricane in its
perfect power.

Maya Angelou

No painter's brush,
nor poet's pen
In justice to her fame
Has ever reached
half high enough
To write a mother's name.

Anonymous

Of all the rights of women, the greatest is to be a mother.

Lin Yutang

There are times when parenthood seems nothing but feeding the mouth that bites you.

Peter De Vries

No matter how old a
mother is, she watches
her middle-aged children
for signs of improvement.

Florida Scott-Maxwell

Don't worry about the
world coming to an
end today. It's already
tomorrow in Australia.

Charles M. Schulz

Cleaning up with
children around
is like shovelling
during a blizzard.

Anonymous

I couldn't live without my music, man. Or me mum.

Robbie Williams

All that I am or ever
hope to be, I owe to
my angel mother.

Abraham Lincoln

Biology is the least
of what makes
someone a mother.

Oprah Winfrey

A mother's happiness is
like a beacon, lighting up
the future but reflected
also on the past in the
guise of fond memories.

Honoré de Balzac

Always laugh
when you can. It is
cheap medicine.

Lord Byron

If there were no schools to take the children away from home… the insane asylums would be filled with mothers.

Edgar Watson Howe

Most children threaten at times to run away from home. This is the only thing that keeps some parents going.

Phyllis Diller

Until I got married, when I used to go out, my mother said goodbye to me as though I was emigrating.

Thora Hird

For the hand that
rocks the cradle
Is the hand that
rules the world.

William Ross Wallace

The hand that rocks the
cradle usually is attached
to someone who isn't
getting enough sleep.

John Fiebig

There is a point at which
you aren't as much mom
and daughter as you are
adults and friends.

Jamie Lee Curtis

If you want your
children to listen,
try talking softly –
to someone else.

Ann Landers

She was the best of
all mothers, to whom,
for body and soul I
owe endless gratitude.

Thomas Carlyle

'Thank God it's Monday.' If any working mother has not experienced that feeling, her children are not adolescent.

Ann Diehl

I cannot tell you how much
I owe to the solemn word
of my good mother.

Charles Haddon Spurgeon

A young lady is a
female child who
has just done
something dreadful.

Judith Martin

Children and mothers
never truly part
Bound in the beating of
each other's heart.

Charlotte Gray

There is a power that
comes to women
when they give birth.

Sheryl Feldman

The pursuit, even
of the best things,
ought to be calm
and tranquil.

Cicero

Imagination is something that sits up with Dad and Mom the first time their teenager stays out late.

Lane Olinghouse

Mother is the heartbeat
in the home; and without
her, there seems to
be no heart throb.

Leroy Brownlow

If you've never
been hated by your
child, you've never
been a parent.

Bette Davis

No influence is so
powerful as that
of the mother.

Sarah Josepha Hale

Womanliness means
only motherhood; all love
begins and ends there.

Robert Browning

They're all mine…
Of course, I'd trade
any of them for
a dishwasher.

Roseanne Barr on her children

A mother always has to
think twice, once for herself
and once for her child.

Sophia Loren

At that best academe,
a mother's knee.

James Russell Lowell

Just do your job
right and your kids
will love you.

Ethel Waters

Govern a family
as you would
cook a small fish
– very gently.

Chinese proverb

I think my life began with
waking up and loving
my mother's face.

George Eliot, *Daniel Deronda*

Stories first heard standing at a mother's knee are never wholly forgotten – a little spring that never quite dries up in our journey through scorching years.

Giovanni Ruffini

The best way to keep children at home is to make the home atmosphere pleasant, and let the air out of the tyres.

Dorothy Parker

All women become
like their mothers.
That is their
tragedy. No man
does. That's his.

Oscar Wilde

Most of all the other
beautiful things in life
come by twos and threes
by dozens and hundreds.
Plenty of roses, stars,
sunsets, rainbows, brothers,
and sisters, aunts and
cousins, but only one
mother in the whole world.

Kate Douglas Wiggin

Oh my son's my son till
he gets him a wife,
But my daughter's my
daughter all her life.

Dinah Craik, 'Young and Old'

Sometimes
the strength of
motherhood is greater
than natural laws.

Barbara Kingsolver

The babe at first feeds upon the mother's bosom, but is always on her heart.

Henry Ward Beecher

Calm parents hear more.
Low-key, accepting parents
are the ones whose children
keep talking to them.

Mary Pipher

The joys of
motherhood are never
fully experienced
until the children
are in bed.

Anonymous

I got my figure back after giving birth. Sad, I'd hoped to get somebody else's.

Caroline Quentin

I think it's a mother's duty
to embarrass their children.

Cher

Raising a kid is
part joy and part
guerrilla warfare.

Ed Asner

Motherhood is a
wonderful thing –
what a pity to waste
it on children.

Judith Pugh

A man loves his sweetheart
the most, his wife the best,
but his mother the longest.

Irish proverb

My mother had a
great deal of trouble
with me, but I think
she enjoyed it.

Mark Twain

Now I have seven children and only one theory: love them, especially when they least deserve to be loved.

Kate Samperi

Raising children is like making biscuits: it is as easy to raise a big batch as one, while you have your hands in the dough.

Edgar Watson Howe

Everybody wants
to save the earth;
nobody wants to help
Mom with the dishes.

P. J. O'Rourke

Being a mother
has made my
life complete.

Darcey Bussell

Many a calm river begins
as a turbulent waterfall, yet
none hurtles and foams
all the way to the sea.

Mikhail Lermontov

There never was a child so lovely, but his mother was glad to get him asleep.

Ralph Waldo Emerson

The story of a
mother's life:
Trapped between a
scream and a hug.

Cathy Guisewite, *Like
Mother, Like Daughter*

Loving a baby is a
circular business…
The more you give
the more you get.

Penelope Leach

Children are a great comfort
in your old age – and they
help you reach it faster, too.

Lionel Kauffman

No animal is so
inexhaustible as
an excited infant.

Amy Leslie

To a child's ear, 'mother' is magic in any language.

Arlene Benedict

Kids can be a pain in the
neck when they're not
a lump in your throat.

Barbara Johnson

Those who say they
'Sleep like a baby'
haven't got one.

Anonymous

There was never a
great man who had
not a great mother.

Olive Schreiner

What do we live for, if it is not to make life less difficult for each other?

George Eliot

There is nothing more
thrilling in this world, I
think, than having a child
that is yours, and yet is
mysteriously a stranger.

Agatha Christie

Youth fades; love
droops; the leaves
of friendship fall;
A mother's secret
hope outlives them all.

Oliver Wendell Holmes Sr

Heaven is at the
feet of mothers.

Arabic proverb

The truth is that parents
are not really interested in
justice. They just want quiet.

Bill Cosby

When a child needs a
mother to talk to, nobody
else but a mother will do.

Erica Jong

Motherhood is perhaps the only unpaid position where failure to show up can result in arrest.

Mary Kay Blakely, *American Mom*

As a parent you try to
maintain a certain amount
of control and so you have
this tug-of-war… You have
to learn when to let go.

Aretha Franklin

Families with
babies and families
without are so sorry
for each other.

Edgar Watson Howe

Smooth seas do not
make skilful sailors.

African proverb

She would tell me Adam
was the rough draft and
Eve was the final product.

Daphne Zuniga on her mother

Mothers are fonder than
fathers of their children
because they are more
certain they are their own.

Aristotle

Only mothers can
think of the future
– because they
give birth to it in
their children.

Maxim Gorky

Parents learn a lot from
their children about
coping with life.

Muriel Spark

A mother's arms
are more comforting
than anyone else's.

Diana, Princess of Wales

You've got to love
your mum more than
yourself, although
I do come a very
close second.

Simon Cowell

No language can express
the power and beauty and
heroism of a mother's love.

Edwin H. Chapin

No one ever died from
sleeping in an unmade bed.

Erma Bombeck

A boy's best friend
is his mother.

Joseph Stefano

A mother is not a person
to lean on, but a person to
make leaning unnecessary.

Dorothy Canfield Fisher

Children are
the only form of
immortality that we
can be sure of.

Peter Ustinov

Motherhood in
all its guises and
permutations is more
art than science.

Melinda M. Marshall

For when a child
is born the mother
also is born again.

Gilbert Parker

It kills you to see
them grow up. But I
guess it would kill you
quicker if they didn't.

Barbara Kingsolver

Motherhood is at its
best when the tender
chords of sympathy
have been touched.

Paul Harris

God could not be everywhere, so he created mothers.

Jewish proverb

Life appears to me too
short to be spent in
nursing animosity, or
registering wrongs.

Charlotte Brontë

The only thing which
seems to me to be
eternal and natural
in motherhood is
ambivalence.

Jane Lazarre

The successful mother
sets her children free
and becomes more free
herself in the process.

Robert J. Havighurst

Having one child
makes you a parent;
having two you
are a referee.

David Frost

Of all the haunting moments
of motherhood, few rank
with hearing your own
words come out of your
daughter's mouth.

Victoria Secunda

To bring up a child in
the way he should go,
travel that way yourself
once in a while.

Josh Billings

I don't approve of smacking – I just use a cattle prod.

Jenny Eclair

If evolution really works,
how come mothers only
have two hands?

Milton Berle

All motherly love
is really without
reason and logic.

Joan Chen

All things are difficult
before they are easy.

Thomas Fuller

It goes without saying
that you should never
have more children than
you have car windows.

Erma Bombeck

The most beautiful word
on the lips of mankind
is the word 'Mother'.

Khalil Gibran

Wrinkles are
hereditary – parents
get them from
their children.

Doris Day

Housework is what
a woman does that
nobody notices unless
she hasn't done it.

Evan Esar

Beautiful as was
mamma's face, it became
incomparably more
lovely when she smiled,
and seemed to enliven
everything about her.

Leo Tolstoy

You see much more
of your children once
they leave home.

Lucille Ball

Do not take life too
seriously – you will never
get out of it alive.

Elbert Hubbard

I'd like to be the ideal mother, but I'm too busy raising my kids.

Anonymous

All mothers are rich when
they love their children.
There are no poor mothers,
no ugly ones, no old ones.

Maurice Maeterlinck

A sweater is a
garment worn by
a child when the
mother feels chilly.

Barbara Johnson

Parents who are afraid
to put their foot down
usually have children
who step on their toes.

Chinese proverb

There is no velvet so soft as a mother's lap, no rose as lovely as her smile.

Edward Thompson

My mother used to say, 'He who angers you, conquers you!' But my mother was a saint.

Elizabeth Kenny

The most consistent
gift and burden of
motherhood is advice.

Susan Chira

Mother's love is bliss,
is peace, it need not
be acquired, it need
not be deserved.

Erich Fromm

Children are the
anchors that hold
a mother to life.

Sophocles

Our mothers always remain
the strangest, craziest
people we've ever met.

Marguerite Duras

A mother holds her
children's hands for a
while, their hearts forever.

Anonymous

Nothing beats
having this beautiful
child look at me
and say, 'mum'.

Nicole Appleton

A mother is one to whom you hurry when you are troubled.

Emily Dickinson

Any mother could perform
the jobs of several air traffic
controllers with ease.

Lisa Alther

If there must be
trouble, let it be in
my day, that my child
may have peace.

Thomas Paine

Being a working mum is not easy. You have to be willing to screw up at every level.

Jami Gertz

It seems to me that
my mother was
the most splendid
woman I ever knew.

Charlie Chaplin

For most exhausted mums,
their idea of 'working out' is
a good, energetic lie-down.

Kathy Lette

It's extraordinary to
look into a baby's face
and see a piece of your
flesh and your spirit.

Liam Neeson

There's no road map
on how to raise a
family: it's always an
enormous negotiation.

Meryl Streep

An ounce of mother is
worth a ton of priest.

Spanish proverb

The patience of a mother
might be likened to a
tube of toothpaste – it's
never quite all gone.

Anonymous

If the kids are
still alive when
my husband gets
home… then hey,
I've done my job.

Roseanne Barr

Parents… spend half their time wondering how their children will turn out, and the rest… when they will turn in.

Eleanor Graham Vance

Children keep us in check. Their laughter prevents our hearts from hardening.

Queen Rania of Jordan

There is no way to be a
perfect mother, and a million
ways to be a good one.

Jill Churchill

Little children,
headache; big
children, heartache.

Italian proverb

Any suburban mother can
state her role sardonically
enough in a sentence:
it is to deliver children
– obstetrically once and
by car forever after.

Peter De Vries

Mother is the one we
count on for the things
that matter most of all.

Katherine Butler Hathaway

Rule number one is,
don't sweat the small
stuff. Rule number two
is, it's all small stuff.

Dr Robert Eliot

Making the decision to have a child is... forever to have your heart go walking around outside your body.

Elizabeth Stone

Even when freshly
washed and relieved
of all obvious
confections, children
tend to be sticky.

Fran Lebowitz

A woman has two smiles
that an angel might envy:
the smile that accepts a
lover before words are
uttered, and the smile
that lights on the first
born babe, and assures
it of a mother's love.

Thomas C. Haliburton

Children behave
as well as they
are treated.

Jan Hunt

If you must hold yourself
up to your children... hold
yourself up as a warning
and not as an example.

George Bernard Shaw

To me, luxury is to be at home with my daughter; and the occasional massage doesn't hurt.

Olivia Newton-John

There is only one
pretty child in the
world, and every
mother has it.

Chinese proverb

There is no reciprocity.
Men love women, women
love children. Children
love hamsters.

Alice Thomas Ellis

When we long for life…
without difficulties, remind
us that oaks grow strong
in contrary winds.

Peter Marshall

A woman is like a teabag. You can't tell how strong she is until you put her in hot water.

Nancy Reagan

Being a mother is learning
about strengths you
didn't know you had, and
dealing with fears you
didn't know existed.

Linda Wooten

Mothers are all
slightly insane.

J. D. Salinger

KEEP
CALM
AND
DRINK
UP

KEEP CALM AND DRINK UP

£4.99

ISBN: 978 1 84953 102 3

'*In victory, you deserve champagne; in defeat, you need it.*'

Napoleon Bonaparte

BAD ADVICE FOR GOOD PEOPLE

Keep Calm and Carry On, a World War Two government poster, struck a chord in recent difficult times when a stiff upper lip and optimistic energy were needed again. But in the long run it's a stiff drink and flowing spirits that keep us all going.

Here's a book packed with proverbs and quotations showing the wisdom to be found at the bottom of the glass.

ALL
YOU
NEED
IS
LOVE

ALL YOU NEED IS LOVE

£4.99

ISBN: 978 1 84953 130 6

*Love is an irresistible desire
to be irresistibly desired.'*

Robert Frost

HEARTFELT WORDS FOR
STARRY-EYED LOVERS

When John Lennon wrote that 'all you need is love' back in 1967, perhaps he'd been struck by the lovebug himself. Love is a gift, love is an adventure, love is a many-splendoured thing – love is what makes the world go round, so why not spread a little of the sweet stuff right now?

Here's a book packed with quotations that will have you feeling the love in no time.

www.summersdale.com